STARS

KAY ROWLEY

POP WORL

Wayland

POP WORLD

POP CONCERTS

POP CULTS

POP STARS

POP VIDEOS

EDITOR: James Kerr
SERIES DESIGNER: Helen White
COVER: Paula Abdul is one of the most popular stars around. She began her career as a cheerleader with the LA Lakers basketball team.

First published in 1991 by Wayland (Publishers) Ltd
61, Western Road, Hove
East Sussex BN3 1JD

© Copyright 1991 Wayland (Publishers) Ltd

Typeset by Helen White Designs
Printed in Italy by G. Canale & C. S. p. A., Turin.
Bound in Belgium by Casterman S. A.

British Library Cataloguing in Publication Data
Rowley, Kay
  Pop stars.
  1. Pop music–Biographies–Collections
  I. Title II. Series
  781.630922

HARDBACK ISBN 0-7502-0124-X

PAPERBACK ISBN 0-7502-0290-4

CONTENTS

INTRO

TODAY'S POP STARS have become the new royalty, taking the place once occupied by movie stars. Artists like Madonna and Paula Abdul earn millions of pounds from the sale of their records and concert tickets, and can number their fans around the world in billions.

The adulation and financial success associated with popular music is not new however, but the scale on which it happens is. As far back as the 1920s, popular singers like Al Jolson became both rich and famous. The arrival of radio was a major step in the spread of popular music. By the end of the 1930s, over 60 million Americans regularly tuned in to the radio.

After 1939, many radio stations in the northern states of the USA began to play 'race' music - later to be renamed rhythm and blues (R&B) - as well as gospel, traditional blues and South American music. Many listeners who liked so-called 'civilized' music were horrified and thought that this was the beginning of the end. However, for the youth of the USA and later Britain, popular music being brought to a much wider audience marked the beginning of the beginning.

After the Second World War music in the USA was in a ferment. By the early 1950s hillbilly music was transforming itself into rockabilly. Teenagers, who wanted more excitement than listening to a bunch of singers who looked like their parents, were tuning in to R&B shows to hear the likes of Fats Domino and Little Richard. One avid listener was Elvis Presley.

M.C. Hammer is one of today's most successful pop stars.

ELVIS AARON PRESLEY was born on 8 January 1935 in Tupelo, Mississippi. As a boy he won a few talent contests and after the family's move to Memphis, he sang in gospel groups and at local dances. When he showed an aptitude for music, his mother insisted on buying him a guitar even though the family was poor.

Elvis was always a loner and did not have many friends at school. Instead he concentrated on cultivating his own style; growing his sideburns and hair - which he greased into a quiff - and favouring pink jackets and black shirts with turned-up collars.

On the strength of three local hits on the Sun record label, Presley toured the South. The reception he got was rapturous, with girls fighting to touch him and tear at his clothes. His performance of his first single, *Heartbreak Hotel,* on the Jimmy and Tommy Dorsey TV show caused a national sensation, and other prime time TV hosts tripped over themselves to have him on their shows. The one

ABOVE: You can see Elvis' influence on stars of today like George Michael.

LEFT: This picture of Elvis perfectly captures the mean and moody attitude that was part of his appeal.

5

condition was that he should be seen only from his waist up; mid-1950s USA was not ready for 'Elvis the Pelvis'.

Aware of the growing power of television, his manager Colonel Tom Parker had Elvis launch many of his new singles on TV and also signed him to a three-movie contract with Paramount. His first film, *Love Me Tender*, grossed over $4 million in the USA alone. It caused riots in cinemas up and down the UK as fans collapsed in tears or showed their appreciation by ripping the seats!

Between 1956 and 1959, Elvis recorded twenty-one hit singles including *Hound Dog*, which sold over one million copies in just two weeks and stayed in the USA top thirty for over six months. In 1958 Elvis was drafted into the army for two years, but Parker was smart and had stockpiled titles to be released during Elvis' absence.

When Elvis returned, rock and roll had lost its grip and had largely been replaced by pop. Elvis' first stereo album, *Elvis is Back,* released in 1960, was a masterpiece and showed that he had lost none of his power. However, after this he started releasing middle-of-the-road singles; mostly tracks from the three films a year he was beginning to churn out. He looked and sounded in good shape. Sadly it was not to last.

In 1969 he had two big hits with *In The Ghetto* and *Suspicious Minds* and released a good live album using material from his comeback show in Las Vegas. Unfortunately, he could not keep up the momentum and gradually withdrew from the public eye, living a more or less reclusive life on his estate in Memphis. From time to time he would come out of hiding and release a record or appear in Las Vegas, but it was clear that the spark had gone.

Elvis spent his final years surrounded by bodyguards and gave away his money to friends and acquaintances in an aimlessly extravagant way. By the time he died he was worth only a couple of million dollars.

Presley died in 1977 aged only forty-two. As news of his death spread across the world, RCA was unable to cope with the demand for his records. During his life he had sold approximately 500 million records worldwide. By the tenth anniversary of his death that figure had risen to over one and a half billion. (That's over one billion more than Michael Jackson!)

In a way Elvis was a victim of his own versatility, never seeming able to decide what sort of music he liked performing best. There's no doubt that he was badly advised both artistically and financially, and he appears to have been largely unaware that Parker was gambling away most of his profits.

Elvis is a role model on whom many pop singers have based their careers. In the early days, singers like Cliff Richard and France's Johnny Halliday closely copied his style. Later on, artists like P.J. Proby and Shakin' Stevens made careers out of being Elvis sound-alikes. Nick Cave's first influence was undoubtedly Elvis' poor boy image. Elvis remains the archetypal pop star and takes his place alongside Marilyn Monroe and James Dean as one of the icons of twentieth-century youth culture.

THE BEATLES formed while still at school. By the middle of 1960, they were playing in clubs around their home town of Liverpool. In need of a change, they decided to take up the offer of a residency in a Hamburg night-club. It was a tough apprenticeship, and they often played for eight or nine hours at a time to less than appreciative audiences.

On their return to Liverpool they were 'discovered' by record store owner Brian Epstein, who became their first manager. After a lot of rejections from record companies, they were finally signed to Parlophone and released their first single, *Love Me Do*, on 5 October 1962. In no time at all *Love Me Do* became a hit on both sides of the Atlantic, and in just over a year The Beatles had four more hits, including two US and UK number ones, *She Loves You* and *I Want To Hold Your Hand*.

'Beatlemania' was now in full spate. No British act before The Beatles had made a significant impact on the US popular music

THE BEATLES: Foreground ; Ringo Starr. Behind from left to right; John Lennon, Paul McCartney and George Harrison.

THE BEATLES

The Rolling Stones

imitated across Europe and the USA. Their collarless mod jackets were considered the height of fashion, and the high street shoe shops rushed to stock up on pointed-toe black leather boots.

After touring the USA, they made their first full-length feature film, *A Hard Day's Night*. This and their next film *Help!*, were complete departures in contemporary music film-making and were the inspiration for the later Monkees TV series and a lot of early pop videos.

At this point The Beatles' career did an about turn. Most groups start off as rebels, then as they grow older they start calming down. The Beatles worked in reverse. While on tour in the USA in 1966, John Lennon caused a controversy by saying that The Beatles were bigger than God. As a result, radio stations up and down the country banned their records and angry citizens picketed their concerts. Their reputations were further dented when Lennon admitted that he and the rest of the band had taken LSD. At the time, the pop world was in the grip of 'flower power', when the taking of such drugs was seen as beneficial. Many of today's pop stars have

scene, and their success opened the doors for the 'British Invasion', by bands like Gerry & The Pacemakers and The Rolling Stones. At one point in the first half of 1964, The Beatles held the first five positions in the US singles chart and had albums at numbers one and two - a record which has never been equalled.

Although the Establishment still considered their 'moptop' haircuts too long, The Beatles' style was spoken out strongly against the use of drugs.

By now the growing dissent between Lennon and Paul McCartney was becoming a problem, and yet they still managed to make two more excellent albums; *The Beatles (Double White)* and *Abbey Road*. The split up of The Beatles in 1970 was a sad end to what had once been one of the most prolific and talented teams of songwriters the pop world had ever seen.

The Beatles' legacy to pop music is incalculable. They were single-handedly responsible for making the general public realize that pop music was here to stay. The Beatles also made it socially acceptable to be a pop star and received the kind of adulation that was once reserved for movie stars. In interviews they came across as witty, clever and amusing, and did away with the notion that all pop musicians were brainless. They made British pop music a force to

The paisley shirts worn by Ringo and Paul, and Ringo's afghan coat were typical of the late 1960s hippie look.

Some of today's bands, like The Stone Roses, have been influenced by the sounds and styles of the 1960s. Ian Brown's hair-style is similar to those sported by The Beatles in the previous picture.

be reckoned with around the world. The tight security systems surrounding today's pop stars like Madonna began with The Beatles. The hysteria which greeted their appearances was unprecedented, and getting the group in and out of some of their concerts required armoured cars and helicopters.

However, their most important gift was their music. It doesn't matter in what style it's sung or who sings it, it remains timeless. In 1990, many stars came together in Liverpool to pay tribute to John Lennon, including Kylie Minogue, Terence Trent D'Arby and Cyndi Lauper. Some sang Lennon's solo compositions and some performed Beatles' songs, but all of the songs sounded as fresh as the day they were written. About how many other pop stars' music and lyrics can one say that?

WHEN THE JACKSON 5 signed to Motown in 1970, Michael - the youngest of the five brothers - was eleven years old. Even at this age, Michael was a seasoned performer. He had been singing with his brothers for five years, first in talent shows then on the club circuit touring with acts such as The Temptations and Gladys Knight & The Pips. When Diana Ross saw the group on a visit to the Jackson's hometown of Gary, Indiana, she was impressed and immediately recommended them to the Motown boss Berry Gordy. Their first record *I Want You Back*, shot straight to the top of the US charts and reached number two in the UK. It was followed by three more top ten hits in the same year.

Gordy was quick to recognize Michael's superior talent and began to groom him for individual stardom. In 1972 Michael equalled the group's record of four hits in a year. By now, the boys were all legally old enough to tour the UK and the five concerts they gave were greeted with the sort of

MICHAEL

Michael Jackson in the early days of The Jackson 5.

13

hysteria previously reserved for The Beatles.

As a group The Jacksons continued to record top-selling albums, but after 1973 they were not producing hit singles. By 1978, their careers had picked up and they were confident enough to both write and produce their new album *Destiny*, which included two massive hits *Shake Your Body* and *Blame It On The Boogie*. The same year Michael made his screen debut as the scarecrow in *The Wiz,* an updated version of *The Wizard of Oz.*

Janet Jackson has used dance, both in her live act and her videos, as successfully as Michael.

The movie's musical director was jazz musician Quincy Jones, and he and Michael immediately struck up a friendship. The two worked together on *Off The Wall,* Michael's first solo LP for Epic. The album showed just how much he had matured as a singer and writer, handling pop, soul, disco and jazz with equal ease.

The record became a pop landmark. In just over six months, four of the tracks made the US and UK top tens, and for one week Michael had three singles in the US top ten. The album chalked up

sales of over eight million copies world-wide and spent over a year and a half in the album charts. For *Don't Stop 'Til You Get Enough* Michael received a Grammy for best male R&B performance.

To follow such an enormous success called for something extra special and it took Michael over three years to come up with it. Released just before Christmas 1982, *Thriller* proved to be a world beater. It is a superb collection of hit songs, brilliantly co-produced by Michael and Quincy Jones. But its success is also due to one of the best marketing campaigns ever mounted for any product. Just when sales looked as though they were starting to level out, promotional ploys helped to extend its shelf life.

By the end of December the first single taken from the album - Michael's duet with McCartney, *The Girl is Mine* - had sold a million, as had the album. To accompany the next two singles, *Billie Jean* and *Beat It*, Michael made two excellent promotional videos showing off his brilliant dance routines. Through the medium of the newly-opened MTV channel in the USA, he captured a whole new audience of fans.

In May, as the album started to descend, 50 million Americans watched Michael perform *Billie Jean* on the Motown twenty-fifth anniversary TV special, and once more *Thriller* hit the number one spot. By November 1983 it had sold ten million copies in the USA

A scene from the video for Billie Jean, *which features one of Michael's most famous dance routines.*

Michael adopted a hard, aggressive image for the Bad *album and tour.*

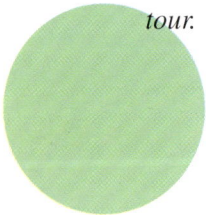

routine. During the next three months the album sold seven and a half million more copies and the video *Making Michael Jackson's 'Thriller'* became the most successful home video ever.

The awards and accolades seemed never-ending. In January 1984, Michael collected seven American Music Awards and in February, eight Grammys. Both records are still unbroken. The LP's total of five top five singles and seven top ten singles has also gone into the record books. The LP rates as the largest selling album ever, with more than 150 gold and platinum discs around the world to its credit. By the end of 1987 world-wide sales had passed the 40 million mark.

1984 saw Michael once again united with his brothers for the 'Victory' tour of the USA and Canada, sponsored by Pepsi Cola. As part of the deal Michael made an advert for the company, but during the shooting he received second-degree burns to his scalp and was rushed to hospital. During 1985, he worked with his old friend Lionel Richie. Together they wrote *We Are The World* for the USA For Africa charity, the USA's answer to Bob Geldof's Band Aid.

alone, but the release of the *Thriller* video put sales into overdrive. Instead of the usual three-minute video, Michael used movie producer John Landis to make a fourteen-minute-long spoof horror film. Special effects and make-up transformed Michael first into a werewolf and then into a zombie, for an inspired dance

By the time *Bad* was released in September 1987, Michael had already completed two of the promotional videos for the album. As it hit the streets, the massive Jackson promotional machine once again went into action, and Michael announced that his first ever solo world-tour would begin in Japan. Throwing off his previous overgrown-teenage outfits, he appeared in a black leather suit and proclaimed himself to have grown up at last.

Michael Jackson was undoubtedly the megastar of the 1980s. He is a unique entertainer who is not afraid to try something new and exciting. However, it seems that the more popular he becomes, the more he shies away from publicity about his private life. Unfortunately, this only serves to make everything he does newsworthy.

As a long-time vegetarian he has let it be known that he would rather live with animals than eat them, and shares his fortified mansion and grounds with his pets. Also, he has increasingly withdrawn from his family. In another attempt to distance himself from his past, he has spent many thousands of dollars restructuring his looks so that he bears little resemblance to the pudgy-faced boy who was in The Jackson 5.

Since Michael Jackson no longer needs the money, he must find other inspirations to keep on making records. But even if he stops tomorrow, he has already joined the pop gods.

Compare this picture of Michael Jackson to the picture of Michael as a boy. He has lightened his skin and straightened his hair.

MADONNA

EVERY NOW AND then a pop star emerges who shines brighter than the rest, who does everything with a little more panache. At first it was not evident that Madonna would be a star of such magnitude, merely another 'one-act disco dolly'. (The quote is her own.) However, by the time the movie *Desperately Seeking Susan* opened in 1985, it had become clear that she had a special talent that was not just limited to making popular, best selling records.

For one thing she was prepared to take risks, shocking people if necessary - as she did with her *Like A Virgin* video. Then, just when everyone thought they had her pinned, she did a complete about turn. From the punk seductress wearing an outsize crucifix, she transformed herself into an elegant Marilyn Monroe look-alike for her *Material Girl* video.

She already had a reputation for being difficult. Some of this was undoubtedly part of her self-publicity campaign, but a lot is due to the fact that she does not suffer fools gladly. She has always been rebellious - a natural reaction, as she sees it, to her strict Roman Catholic upbringing.

The punky look Madonna adopted for the film Desperately Seeking Susan *was copied by many of her fans.*

Madonna's mother died when Madonna was young, and her father later remarried. Unfortunately she and her new stepmother did not get along. She was already keen to take up dancing as a career and knew she would have to look beyond her home town of Detroit to get more experience. As soon as she could, she left home and went to New

York, a brave move for a seventeen year old with only $35 to her name.

She loved New York and stayed for two years, performing with dance troupes and acting in several underground movies. However, to make ends meet she had to hold down other jobs, including working in a doughnut diner and posing for art classes. After a brief spell in Paris, she returned to New York and threw herself into music, teaching herself to play drums, guitar and keyboards. While playing in a number of bands, she took the demo tapes of her own songs around the clubs until at last, in 1982, she was signed up as a solo artist by Sire Records.

After one false start, she let loose a string of hits which has continued unabated to the present day. In the UK alone she has had seven number one singles, twenty-five top fives and three number one LPs. In the USA, not only has she become the top-selling female artist of all time, but her run of seventeen consecutive top five hits shattered the record previously held by The Beatles.

For most pop stars this would be more than enough, but for Madonna it is patently not. The more she achieves, the more she pushes herself to new heights. She stopped needing the money long ago, so what is the spur? Perhaps the closest answer comes from an interview in which she is quoted as saying, 'I always said I wanted to be famous. . . I never said I wanted to be rich.'

Prince, like Madonna, has made the transition from music to film. The two stars worked together on Madonna's Like A Prayer *album.*

RIGHT: Madonna as she appeared in the film Dick Tracy.

OPPOSITE: Madonna used ultra-trendy designer Jean-Paul Gaultier to design her clothes for the 'Blonde Ambition' tour.

BELOW: Neneh Cherry, like Madonna, has become a female pop star on her own terms.

Unkind critics would say that she's already famous for being famous. Her marriage to actor Sean Penn, who is known for having an equally short fuse, was conducted in the full glare of media publicity. Penn's fights with paparazzi photographers, and the couple's several break and make-ups have been publicized world-wide.

Madonna's run-ins with the press whenever she goes out jogging with her platoon of bodyguards are all part of the act. Recently she was in the news when her name was linked with that of actor Warren Beatty, her co-star in the movie *Dick Tracy*.

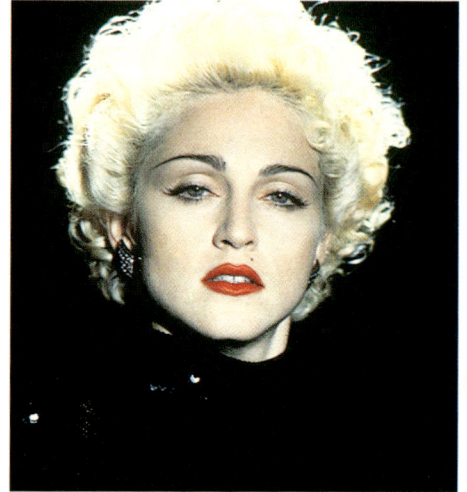

If, however, she wants to be famous as an actress, she still has a long way to go. After *Desperately Seeking Susan,* her best performances have all been reserved for her videos and her concerts. On the pop side she continues to amaze, and her latest 'Blonde Ambition' tour is typical of her 'all or nothing' approach to her art. It is an elaborately-choreographed extravaganza, with special effects and epic sets against which Madonna - in outrageous costumes designed by Jean-Paul Gaultier, and supported by a band, singers and dancers - struts her stuff. Whatever she attempts in the future, there is no question that for the 1980s at least, she was a major influence on pop, fashion and youth culture.

KYLIE & JASON

UNTIL RECENTLY, AUSTRALIA had not been prominent in its contribution to the international pop scene. For one thing, it is too far away from the hub of pop music - the USA and the UK. As a result, many talented musicians have had to be content with being national rather than international stars. Those artists who have made it, INXS for example, have done so by moving westwards.

With Kylie and Jason the story is somewhat different. They had already established themselves as TV personalities in the UK without ever having left Australia. Achieving acceptance as pop stars, therefore, was that much easier. Kylie also had a number one record to her credit with a remake of the Little Eva hit *The Locomotion* - Australia's biggest selling single of 1987.

Both Jason and Kylie have been acting since they were children. At the age of eleven Kylie appeared in an episode of the soap opera *Skyways*, which is where she first met Jason. Both went on to have a

succession of TV roles, around which they had to accommodate their schooling. Because of his father's insistence that he keep up his studies, Jason originally turned down a part in a new series called *Neighbours*! As it turned out, the series was dropped after six months then picked up again by another network, with Jason taking over the part of Scott Robinson. Cast opposite him was Kylie Minogue as his girlfriend Charlene.

Over the next year and a half the series became a huge hit, with the relationship between Scott and Charlene emerging as the main attraction for both Australian and British audiences. Although *Neighbours* was launched simultaneously in the UK, it was relegated to a mid-morning slot. However, soon after Kylie joined the show it became a firm favourite with schoolchildren.

When she was growing up, Kylie's favourite singer was Agnetha from Abba, and she dreamed of one day becoming just as famous. After the success of her Australian hit record, she decided to take the plunge and go to London to follow it up. On first meeting her, hit songwriters Stock, Aitken and Waterman (S.A.W.)

were sceptical and thought 'she should be so lucky' as to have a hit. The rest is, as they say, hysteria!

I Should Be So Lucky shot to number one in the UK and Australia and became a hit in sixteen other countries where no-

ABOVE: The Australian rockers, INXS.

OPPOSITE: Kylie is popular because of her 'girl next door' image.

23

one had even heard of *Neighbours*. In the next two and a half years she clocked up nine more hit singles, including three more number ones and five number twos.

Meanwhile Jason had also decided to launch himself as a pop singer and followed in Kylie's footsteps with another S.A.W. song, *Nothing Can Divide Us*. By now Kylie and Jason were Britain's favourite couple, a fairy-tale prince and princess of pop, so a duet seemed a golden opportunity not to be missed. *Especially For You* became an enormous hit, spending three weeks at number one in November 1988 and selling just under a million records.

ABOVE: Kylie and Jason.

RIGHT: For today's pop stars, even a Christmas shopping trip can turn into a media event.

OPPOSITE: Like many pop stars before her, Kylie Minogue has gone on to star in feature films such as The Delinquents.

When Jason went on the road the next spring, he and everyone else were taken aback by the overwhelming reception he got from devoted fans. Thousands queued to see him and the press likened the reaction to Beatlemania. That year Jason was voted best male singer, best-dressed person and most fanciable male by pop fans in the UK.

By the beginning of 1989, both Kylie and Jason had left *Neighbours* to concentrate on their pop careers, shrewd enough to know that they should make the most out of their fame before the public got tired of them. Critics frequently carp that anyone could sing their songs and have a hit, and that Jason and Kylie are so ordinary. However, this is exactly their appeal. They are ordinary, like the perfect boy and girl next door in any street.

Becoming a pop star via television exposure is not new. What makes Jason and Kylie different is that they have emerged in more sophisticated times. They can draw on the experience of others to guide them through the minefield of instant megastardom and avoid being has-beens by the age of twenty-five.

NEW KIDS

THE STORY OF New Kids On The Block reads just like a fairy-tale; five young white boys from a tough neighbourhood in Boston, Massachusetts become instant pop megastars. The reality is that it took them five years of hard work to achieve 'overnight' success, master-minded by a record producer, Maurice Starr, whose aim it was to put together a group which would appeal to both black and white kids. Starr had already worked with the group New Edition and by mid-1985 he had come up with five talented teenagers who could sing, dance and rap in a crossover style. Giving them the improbable name of Nynuk, he tried them out before a huge black audience at an open-air festival, figuring that if they could be accepted and not lose their nerve there, they could play anywhere.

By January 1986 he had secured them a recording contract, and during the course of the year they released two singles and a creditable if unspectacular LP. The reaction from DJs and the press had been polite but mostly unenthusiastic, so it was back to the drawing board.

The New Kids have adopted a look that was popularized by black rappers: Hi-tops, sweat-shirts and peace medallions.

Through the first half of 1987 they worked hard to perfect their dance routines and new songs, and once again Starr decided to put them to the test. Though they were local heroes they still meant nothing outside Boston, so he deliberately chose the most difficult crowd he could think of; the notoriously hard-to-please, predominantly black audience at the Apollo Theatre in Harlem, New York. In the event they received a standing ovation and were now ready to take on all-comers.

With the release of their second album, *Hangin' Tough*, everything finally started to come together.

The single *Please Don't Go Girl* made the US top ten and there was immediate talk of a nation-wide tour supporting Tiffany. There was still the matter of their school work to consider but it seemed too good a chance to turn down.

So started a punishing tour and recording schedule which has continued uninterrupted for the last two and a half years, and has earned them the title 'the five hardest-working kids in show business'. After the first leg of the Tiffany tour, they embarked on a small headlining tour of their own, taking time-out to go to Japan to make an advert for Sony.

Since leaving New Edition – producer Maurice Starr's first teen vocal-group – Bobby Brown has enjoyed phenomenal success.

The New Kids On The Block. From left to right: Jon, Jordan, Joe, Danny and Donnie.

Following the second half of the Tiffany tour, they took off for Hawaii to play dates there over Christmas and the New Year.

In 1989 all their hard work was rewarded. They became the first teen vocal-group to rack up four top ten hits from one album, which itself went on to sell over eight million copies. By summer they were still playing relatively small venues, but this time with Tiffany supporting them. So many heart-broken fans were being turned away that another tour was immediately put together, this time with the concerts taking place in 10,000 – 15,000-seater stadiums.

By September they had completed more than 100 dates across the USA, with hardly a minute to draw breath. Even their Christmas album had to be recorded on the road using a mobile unit from their Boston recording studio, House of Hits. Their one hour and forty minutes show of non-stop songs, raps, dance routines, jokes and impersonations was perfect material for a video. Since its release at the end of last year, *Hangin' Tough Live* has sold almost two million copies.

Having conquered the USA, in 1990 they briefly turned their attention to Europe. They planned to capitalize on their belated record success in Europe with a mini-tour of the UK. As a controlled experiment it was highly effective: tickets for the concerts sold out almost immediately and they encountered the by-now-usual fan hysteria. Unfortunately for European fans, however prestigious it may be for US acts to do well in Europe, the real money is still to be made in the USA, playing the giant stadia which seat 50,000 plus. So for the rest of 1990, the Kids' tour schedule went on its gruelling way, playing ever-larger venues.

Their video for *Step By Step* showed that they were growing up quickly, and Donnie Wahlberg, the self-appointed leader, has stepped outside the group to duet with Japanese pop megastar Seiko. How long the Kids stay together will depend on how much artistic freedom they are allowed and how quickly they tire of being closeted together, living most of the year in tour buses and hotels away from their families and friends. For the time being, they have enough exciting new projects to engross and enrich them; a full-length feature film, a TV cartoon series and a recently signed $3 million deal with Coca-Cola.

The New Kids' image has always been based on 'what you see is what you get'; they are straightforward, uncomplicated teenagers whose passion is music. By great good luck, they have been allowed to pursue their hobby for a living. Their concern for young people not as fortunate as themselves seems genuine, and they have, as Governor Dukakis of Boston puts it, 'used their popularity as a platform' to speak out against drugs and racism. As potential role models for many of their young fans, they are aware of how important their public statements are and how different their own lives could have been.

Another artist who has brought rap into the mainstream is Monie Love.

GLOSSARY

Adulation   Excessive flattery or praise.

Archetypal   The perfect example of a particular thing.

Blues   A type of folk music which originated among black Americans.

Choreographed   To have had dance steps arranged.

Composition   A piece of music with or without words.

Co-produced   Produced with another person.

Crossover   Appealing to white as well as black audiences.

Flower power   A youth movement of the late 1960s which celebrated peace and love and which was associated with drug taking.

Gospel music   Religious music which originated in the black churches of southern USA.

Grammy   A US music-award.

Hillbilly music   Another name for pre-rock and roll American country music.

Hysteria   Wild excitement.

Icon   An image which has a special or sacred meaning.

Middle-of-the-road music   Traditional popular music.

Mod   Relating to the fashion in clothing of the early to mid-1960s in the UK.

'Moptop'   A haircut which was characterized by a long fringe and which was made fashionable by The Beatles.

Motown   A record label specializing in soul music, formed in Detroit in the 1960s.

Panache   Style.

Paparazzi   Journalists and photographers who follow the stars around.

Picketed   Protested against by people who try to prevent other people from entering a building, for example.

Promotional   Relating to methods used to increase the sale of a product.

Punk   Fashion or music of the late 1970s characterized by ripped clothing and aggressive music.

Quiff   A hairstyle that was fashionable among teenage boys in the 1950s, where the hair was brushed above the forehead.

'Race' music   The label given by white-owned record companies to music performed by black Americans before the 1950s.

Rhythm and blues   Music originally performed by black Americans. It was influenced by the blues but usually had a stronger beat.

Rockabilly   Energetic white American country music. It was a forerunner of rock and roll.

Sponsored   Supported, usually by a firm or business, with money.

Spoof   A humorous imitation.

Stadia   The plural of stadium.

The Establishment   A group or class of people which has authority within a society. It is identified as having traditional views.

Underground movie   A movie which is experimental and is produced by independent film makers.

Youth culture   The total range of activities, ideas, fashions, and tastes of young people.

READING LIST

Elvis in His Own Words edited by Mick Farren (W.H. Allen, 1981)

Kylie The Superstar Next Door by Sasha Stone (Omnibus/MBI, 1990)

Madonna In Her Own Words by Mick St. Michael (Omnibus, 1980)

Michael Jackson: Body And Soul by Geoff Brown (Virgin, 1984)

Motown The History by Sharon Davis (Guinness, 1988)

New Kids On The Block: The Whole Story By Their Friends (Robin McGibbon, 1990)

Pop Music by Matt and Fiona Wallis (Wayland, 1989)

The Beatles: A Day In The Life compiled by Tom Schultheiss (Omnibus, 1980)

The Pop Music Business by Phillip Hayward (Wayland, 1988)

PICTURE ACKNOWLEDGEMENTS

All Action Pictures (L. Cotteral) 4, 26; London Features International 15, (R. J. Capak) 17, 22; Relay Photos Ltd (Justin Thomas) 7, (Chris Walter) 9, 11, (Justin Thomas) 12, 13, 16, 21, 25, (Andre Csillag) 28, (Justin Thomas) 29; Rex Features Limited 5 (bottom and top), 6, 8, 10, (Peter Brooker) 19, (Nils Jorgensen) 20 (bottom), 24 (top), (Nils Jorgensen) 24 (Bottom), (Todd Gray) 27; Touchstone Pictures (Peter Sore) 20 (top); Warner Bros. 18.

READING LIST

INDEX